Date: 5/4/15

MEET THE
ANCIENT
ROMANS

Alex Woolf

Gareth Stevens
PUBLISHING

Please visit our website, **www.garethstevens.com**. For a free color catalog of all our high-quality books, call toll free 1-800-542-2595 or fax 1-877-542-2596.

Woolf, Alex.
Meet the ancient Romans / by Alex Woolf.
p. cm. — (Encounters with the past)
Includes index.
ISBN 978-1-4824-0904-8 (pbk.)
ISBN 978-1-4824-0887-4 (6-pack)
ISBN 978-1-4824-0886-7 (library binding)
1.Rome — Civilization — Juvenile literature. 2. Rome — Social life and customs — Juvenile literature.
I. Woolf, Alex, 1964- II. Title.
DG78.W66 2015
937—d23

First Edition

Published in 2015 by
Gareth Stevens Publishing
111 East 14th Street, Suite 349
New York, NY 10003

Editors: Joe Harris and Nicola Barber
Design: Elaine Wilkinson
Cover design: Elaine Wilkinson

Cover pictures Shutterstock: Colosseum Leoks;
soldier James Steidl; coin Keith Wheatley; amphora Kaband.

Picture acknowledgements: Alamy: p26 Carlos Mora. The Bridgeman Art Library: p17 top Private
Collection/The Stapleton Collection. Britannia (www.durolitum.co.uk): p10, p11 bottom.
Corbis: p19 bottom Araldo de Luca; p22 Francesco Iacobelli/JAI; p25 top National Geographic Society.
Getty Images: p17 bottom Giorgio Cosulich. Guarderobe (www.guarderobe.co.uk): p6, p12, p13 bottom,
p24. iStock: p14 Selimaksan.Shutterstock: p4 background Khunaspix, inset top Pres Panayotov, coins
left Claudio Divizia, middle left Paul Picone, middle right and right KA Photography KEVM111, pouch
Scott Rothstein; pp5 and 28 Federico Rostagno; pp6-7 Viacheslav Lopatin; p7 top Tomasz Szymanski;
p7 bottom Benedictus; p8 Algol; p9 top Peter Lorimer; pp10-11 and title page Pres Panayotov; p11 top
Arena Photo UK; pp12-13 Renata Sedmakova; p13 top and 22-3 Bertl123; pp14-15 RnDmS; p15 top
Sasimoto; p15 bottom Luigi Nifosi; pp16-17 Mountainpix; p16 Vladimir Korostyshevskiy; pp18-19
Alena Stalmashonak; pp20-21 Jaime Pharr; p20 and title page StockPhotoAstur; p21 top Meunierd;
p21 bottom Pavila; p23 top NCG; p23 bottom Mountainpix; pp24-5 Evgeny Mogilnikov; p25 bottom
Mountainpix; pp26-7, 27 top and contents Motordigitaal; p29 eZeePics Studio. Wikimedia Commons:
pp8-9 Patrick Denker; p9 bottom Ad Meskens; p18 Amparo Cardona; p19 top J. Patrick Fischer; p27
and title page Luis García; p28 Jean-Pol Grandmont.

Printed in the United States of America

CPSIA compliance information: Batch CS15GS: For further information contact Gareth Stevens, New York, New York at 1-800-542-2595.

Contents

Into the Past

You run along the empty school hallway. You're late for your class. The history teacher is strict – you're going to be in trouble. Suddenly, right in front of you, a door appears. There are no walls around it – it's just a plain, wooden door in the middle of the hallway.

You stand there, amazed. Then, without thinking, you open the door. You find yourself in a small room with a stone floor and white walls. On a table in the middle of the room is a pile of clothing, a leather pouch containing coins, and a wax tablet with these words scrawled on it:

▲ Janus was the Roman god of doorways and passages. He was usually shown with two heads, facing both to the past and to the future.

Your Mission

You are about to enter the city of Rome. The year is 83 CE, the second year of the reign of the Emperor Domitian. Your mission is to meet people and find out about their lives. The mission will last six hours.

At that moment, another door in the opposite wall starts to open. Bright sunlight floods the room. You can hear the cries of street traders and the squeak of cartwheels. There are smells of cooking meat and horse manure. Quickly, you put on the tunic, cloak, and sandals from the pile and grab the money pouch. Then you take a deep breath, and walk through the open door…

Helping the Senator

Y ou find yourself in ancient Rome. You are standing in the Forum – a huge space surrounded by the pillared entrances of temples and government buildings, and teeming with life. As you start to look round, you are stopped by a senator. He asks if you can help him find a missing girl. He offers to pay you, but you say you'll help him for free if he'll answer some questions.

IS THIS AN IMPORTANT CITY?

Rome is the most important city in the known world, the capital of a vast empire that extends from North Africa to Britain, and from Spain to Judea. The city you see around you is largely the work of the Emperor Augustus, who died in 14CE. He built magnificent temples, palaces, public baths, and monuments, paid for by taxes raised from the provinces of our empire.

WHO RUNS THE EMPIRE?

Not us senators, that's for sure. We used to be powerful, but these days real power lies with the emperor. We've had good emperors, like Augustus, and really bad ones, like Caligula. Wise emperors don't flaunt their power, but respect the rights of citizens. All emperors try to stay popular by keeping the population of Rome supplied with food and entertained by public games.

HAS ROME ALWAYS BEEN IMPORTANT?

No. Rome began as a small place. According to legend it was founded in 753BCE. Romulus was the city's first king. The Romans became increasingly wealthy and powerful as they conquered rival kingdoms in Italy and beyond. After a succession of kings, the citizens overthrew the monarchy in 509BCE and established a republic, governed by the Senate. The republic lasted until 27BCE. We've been ruled by emperors since then.

According to legend, as babies Romulus and his twin brother, Remus, were rescued and cared for by a she-wolf, after being abandoned in the Tiber River.

Snacks from the Street Vendor

The senator said the girl is wearing a red tunic and has short, blonde hair – she is from Germania. You glimpse a girl in red dash down one of the bustling side streets. You follow and find yourself in a crowded market filled with stalls and taverns selling delicious-smelling hot and cold snacks. Feeling hungry, you go to one of the stalls and speak to the vendor.

WHAT CAN I BUY HERE?

At this stall you can buy salted bread, eggs, smoked cheese, or figs. Or, if you want a hot meal, try one of the taverns. They're called *popinae* and they sell hot sausages, pies, soups, stews, and baked cheese covered in honey. You can even sit at a table to eat in the *popinae* – but my food is cheaper!

WHY IS STREET FOOD SO POPULAR? DOES NO ONE COOK AT HOME?

Most ordinary citizens of Rome don't have kitchens. They live in small flats in tall apartment blocks. Some of these blocks, called *insulae*, are up to seven stories high. The better flats have running water and a hearth, but the cheaper ones on the upper floors don't. Anyway, the likelihood of starting a fire makes it too risky to cook food in one of those buildings.

WHERE DOES THE FOOD COME FROM?

Grain for the city's bread comes mostly from Sicily and North Africa. Fruit and vegetables are grown on big farm estates called *latifundiae* in the surrounding countryside. Oil, wine, olives, and dates come from southern Italy and Greece. Spices arrive on merchant ships from the East.

Pottery containers called *amphorae* were used throughout the ancient Roman world to transport wine, oil, and other foodstuffs.

Talking to the Net Man

After your snack, you join the crowd going into the newly built Colosseum, ready to enjoy an afternoon at the games. You spy the girl in red entering through a gate. You follow and find yourself heading down some steps into the *hypogeum*, a network of rooms and tunnels beneath the amphitheater. A gladiator is there, so you ask him some questions.

WHAT KIND OF GLADIATOR ARE YOU?

I am a *retiarius*, or net man. I fight with a net, a trident, and a dagger. I don't wear a helmet or much armor, which means I'm light on my feet, but not well protected. I usually fight the *secutor*, who wears a helmet and some armor. He carries a shield for protection and fights with a sword.

WHY DID YOU CHOOSE THIS DANGEROUS LIFE?

I didn't choose it! I was born in Germania and was captured in war. I was brought here and forced to train as a gladiator in the *ludus*, or training school. I'm bound to service by a sacred oath, and I've been branded – see here – on my hand. Still, it's not such a bad life. We eat well and get decent medical care.

This gladiator is named Lytras. He has a short, curved sword and is protected by armor and a shield. The figure in white is the referee.

WHAT WILL HAPPEN TO YOU?

Well, I hope to win my fight today! If I lose, that could mean death. The spectators will decide. If the defeated gladiator fights well and bravely, they usually spare his life. I've won my first three contests. If I keep winning, my master may eventually grant me my freedom. That's my dream...

The *secutor* was better protected than the *retiarius*, but his heavy metal helmet made fighting very hard work.

The Busy Surgeon

You ask the gladiator if he's seen a girl in a red tunic. He says she used to come to the *hypogeum* occasionally with the senator and his wife. He doesn't know why she came back here, but he saw her talking to the surgeon just now. So you go to the medical room of the Colosseum in search of the surgeon. You find him tending to a wounded gladiator. As he works, you ask him questions.

DO YOU USE MEDICINES?

Yes, after I have operated I use unwashed wool dipped in wine or vinegar to help heal wounds. For dysentery, I recommend yolks of eggs mixed with the ashes of their shells, poppy juice, and wine. Garlic is good for the heart, fenugreek cures lung disease, and I always prescribe boiled liver to patients with sore eyes.

HOW DO YOU CURE THE SICK?

We Romans believe it's important not to get sick in the first place! That's why we've built aqueducts to supply fresh running water to our cities, public bathhouses to encourage people to wash regularly, and sewage systems to carry away our waste. We believe this helps to keep disease at bay.

The Romans built aqueducts to carry clean water to their towns and cities.

WHAT KIND OF OPERATIONS DO YOU CARRY OUT?

At the amphitheater, and on the battlefield, I wash and stitch up all kinds of injuries. I use bone drills and forceps to remove objects such as arrowheads from deep wounds. Sometimes I even have to amputate arms or legs! I also perform simpler operations such as cutting off warts and growths, or pulling out rotten teeth.

The Bathhouse Keeper

The surgeon explains that the girl is a slave, and she ran away from the senator because he was cruel to her. She came back here hoping for a job. The surgeon told her they were looking for attendants at the bathhouse nearby. After the hot, sweaty *hypogeum*, a trip to the bathhouse seems like a good idea. But when you get there, you find yourself in a maze of rooms. It's very confusing. You ask the advice of the bathhouse keeper.

WHICH ROOM SHOULD I GO TO FIRST?

You should start in the warm room, or *tepidarium*. Here you can lie on a table while a slave gives you a massage with oil. After that, you should move to the hot room, or *caldarium*. When you are really sweaty, a slave will scrape the oil, sweat, and dirt off your body. Finally you take a plunge in the cold pool, or *frigidarium*.

14

HOW ARE THE BATHS HEATED?

The baths are heated by the hot air from a furnace. The floors of the baths are raised off the ground, held up by pillars of tiles. Hot air from the furnace passes through the spaces between the pillars, and heats the floors above. It also passes through spaces in the walls. This heating system is called a *hypocaust*. The furnace is closest to the *caldarium*, which is why that room is the warmest.

ARE THE BATHS JUST FOR BATHING?

No, not at all! This is a whole leisure complex. As well as bathing, you can exercise with weights, take part in sports, such as wrestling, have a massage, read in the library, buy a snack, shop for gifts, or take a walk in the gardens. Women visit in the mornings with their children, while men come in the afternoons after work.

Exercising and playing games were part of a visit to the Roman baths.

15

The Senator's Wife

The senator you saw earlier is having a massage. He tells you that the slave girl has been found and returned to him. He invites you to a banquet at his house. You decide to go – it's your only chance to help the girl. After arriving at the house, you enter the dining hall, or triclinium, and take a seat on a couch next to the senator's wife. You talk to her.

HOW DO YOU SPEND YOUR DAY?

While my husband goes out to work, I am in charge of the household. I decide on the menu for the evening meal and send the slaves to the market to buy food. Later in the morning, I meet with friends at the public baths. In the afternoons, I may make an offering at the temple, watch the debates at the Forum, or visit the games.

DO YOU SPEND A LOT OF TIME ON YOUR APPEARANCE?

Endless hours! After bathing, slaves rub my skin with pumice stones to remove body hair and dead skin. They pluck my eyebrows, then tie up my hair with ribbons. They use chalk to whiten my face and rouge made of lead to color my cheeks and highlight my eyes.

ARE YOU AS FREE AS YOUR HUSBAND?

No, I am not a citizen. I cannot vote, or become a senator. But, like all women, my schooling stopped when I was 11 years old, so I don't know much about politics anyway. I could have become a Vestal – a priestess of the Roman goddess Vesta. These priestesses have high status, although they're not allowed to marry or to have children.

At the Banquet

The banquet is delicious, but during the meal, you sneak out of the *triclinium* and make your way to the kitchen, hoping to find the slave girl. The kitchen is hot, smoky, and bustling with activity. Slaves are busy chopping vegetables, grinding spices, or roasting meat on a spit over a fire. The girl is not there, but you take the opportunity to ask the cook some questions.

HOW LONG DO MEALS LAST?

Banquets often have at least six courses and last up to four hours. They begin with cold food, such as eggs, raw vegetables, and fish. These are followed by richer main courses, usually smothered in sauces. You'll be relieved to hear that most meals do not last as long as banquets. Breakfast and lunch are much simpler, shorter meals.

WHAT IS THE MOST SPLENDID DISH YOU'VE EVER SERVED?

I have cooked many elaborate dishes – giant snails in garlic and dormice served in honey sauce. Sometimes I disguise one dish as another, making swans from pastry or roast pork carved in the shape of a fish. But my most masterful creation was a roasted pig with its belly filled with live thrushes. When it was cut open, the birds flew out, surprising the guests.

DO MUSICIANS USUALLY PLAY DURING A BANQUET?

Oh yes, the master likes to have musicians, dancers, poets, and clowns to entertain the guests. Our musicians play on flutes, tambourines, and lyres. Dancers click castanets as they sway to the music. Often, the main dish is carried into the *triclinium* to an accompaniment of music and dancing.

A Roman musician plays a tambourine.

A Soldier's Life

You ask the cook if he knows where the recaptured slave girl might be. He doesn't, but he thinks the senator's son might be able to help you. You go to the son's quarters. He is a military tribune – a senior officer in the Roman army. You ask him if he has a few minutes to answer your questions about the army.

HOW IS THE ROMAN ARMY ORGANIZED?

The Roman army is divided into 30 legions. Each legion has between 3,000 and 6,000 soldiers, most of them foot soldiers. There are ten cohorts of foot soldiers in each legion. The cohorts are divided into centuries, each one made up of 80 men and led by experienced soldiers called centurions.

WHAT IS LIFE LIKE IN THE ARMY?

Most recruits are aged between 18 and 22. They sign up for 25 years of service. When not actually fighting, soldiers are kept occupied with drills, training, route marches, and fort-building exercises. Army life is highly disciplined. Theft, desertion, or cowardice in battle are punishable by death.

WHAT HAPPENS TO SOLDIERS WHEN THEY RETIRE?

The soldiers who live to retirement receive a plot of land, which they can farm, and a regular income. Many who have served for a long time in one of the provinces decide to settle there in their retirement, close to their old military base. They often end up marrying local women.

A Roman centurion.

Meeting the Engineer

The soldier tells you that the slave girl has been sent to her dormitory. As he is speaking, there is a cry of distress from the mistress. "The water has stopped flowing," she complains. "How am I going to wash?" It seems there is a fault in the household plumbing. The engineer is summoned to fix it. As he works, you talk to him about his job.

WHERE DOES THE WATER COME FROM?

The water used in Rome comes a long way. It's brought to the city along channels called aqueducts. The water flows over these long distances down very slight downward slopes, along bridges, and through pipes and tunnels. Rome has 13 aqueducts that supply the public baths, latrines, fountains, and private households of the city.

APART FROM AQUEDUCTS AND SEWERS, WHAT ELSE DO ROMAN ENGINEERS BUILD?

I have helped to build roads, bridges, dams, mines, and buildings all over the empire. We Romans build to last, using materials like brick, stone, cement, concrete, and marble. We make our roads as straight as possible. We prefer to build bridges over waterways or tunnel through hills rather than wind our roads around such obstacles.

WHAT HAPPENS TO WASTE FROM THE LATRINES?

Rome has a network of underground sewers, covered by stones. Some of the aqueducts send water into the latrines. The water washes the waste from the latrines into the sewers. The sewers carry the waste to the city's main drain, the Cloaca Maxima, which empties into the Tiber River.

A Roman surveyor takes measurements for a building project.

Working as a Slave

The engineer tells you that it was he who blocked the water supply in order to get into the house. He is helping a friend – a merchant, whose daughter was kidnapped and sold into slavery. It's the girl you've been searching for all day. You lead him to the slaves' dormitory and, together, you manage to sneak the girl out of the house. You're shocked at how young she is! As you make your escape, you talk to the girl.

WHAT IS A SLAVE'S LIFE LIKE?

I ran away because my master and mistress were often cruel to me. Our masters own us so we are at their mercy. If I ever have children of my own, they will be slaves as well. I've heard that slaves in other houses are treated better than here, though.

DO SLAVES WORK IN OTHER PLACES APART FROM HOUSES?

Oh yes. This empire was built by slaves! Slaves build the roads and aqueducts; they are sent down the mines to dig out gold and silver. They labor on the farms that keep this city fed. Educated slaves are the luckiest. They can earn their own money as teachers, accountants, or physicians.

Roman slaves hard at work stoking a furnace.

ARE SLAVES EVER FREED?

Kind masters often free their slaves eventually. Slaves who have earned some money can buy their freedom. Male slaves who have been freed (freedmen) are able to vote, buy property, and even own slaves of their own, but they aren't citizens so they can't become Roman officials. Their children, however, do become full Roman citizens.

A slave talks to his master and mistress.

At the Temple of Saturn

The engineer takes you and the girl to the Temple of Saturn in the Forum where the girl's father is waiting for her. They are overjoyed to see each other. After she has thanked you, and she and her father have departed, you speak to a priestess in the temple.

WHO ARE THE MAIN GODS?

The most important Roman gods are Jupiter, king of the gods and god of sky and thunder, Mars, god of war, Mercury, the messenger god, Neptune, god of the sea, Venus, goddess of love, and Minerva, goddess of healing. As the empire has grown, we have found new gods to worship, for example in Egypt. Since the time of Emperor Augustus, we've also started worshipping our emperors as gods.

DO ALL TEMPLES LOOK LIKE THIS?

Yes, all the temples throughout the empire are built to the same basic pattern, with a triangular roof supported by pillars. Each temple is dedicated to a particular god or goddess. In the main room of the temple, there is a statue of the god, and an altar for incense or offerings. Animal sacrifices are made at an altar outside the temple.

HOW DO ROMANS WORSHIP?

People come to the temple to make sacrifices or offerings of food, flowers, or money. During festivals, I sacrifice an animal, such as a bull, at the outdoor altar. We Romans also worship at home. Every home has a small altar and shrine containing little statues called *lares*, or household gods, and the whole family worships there every day.

This small bronze statue is one of the *lares* – the household gods.

Back to the Present

The six hours are over. You make your way back to the Forum. There is a bright flash of light and the doorway reappears. You pass through it into the little room where you leave your Roman garments and change back into your own clothes. You pass through the second door and find yourself back in the school hallway. Your history teacher is there, leaning out of the classroom. "You're late!" he says. "Hurry up. Today we're learning all about the Romans!"

WHAT ABOUT ROMAN SLAVES?

You want to know more about the slave girl, and her life. You discover that many Roman slaves were captured in war and bought and sold at slave markets. Others were born to slave parents. Jobs for household slaves included dressing the master or mistress, cooking, cleaning, washing clothes, gardening, and serving the master and guests at dinner. A Roman writer called Seneca believed that a master should treat a slave well because a happy slave would work better.

Seneca the Younger.

WHAT HAPPENED TO ROME?

Rome continued to be the capital of the Roman Empire until 286CE. By then, Rome was important for a different reason – it had become the center of the Roman Catholic religion, and the official home of the head of the Roman Catholic Church, the Pope. Rome was a major center of art and culture during the Renaissance, and since 1871, it has been the capital of Italy.

Glossary

accountant A person who keeps or inspects financial records.

amphitheater A round or oval building, usually without a roof, with a central space where sporting events or theatrical shows are presented. Seats for spectators surround the central space.

aqueduct A channel or bridge for carrying water from a water source to a town or city.

brand To mark an animal or human with a hot iron.

castanets Small hollow pieces of wood, joined in pairs by a cord, and clicked together by the fingers as a rhythmic accompaniment to dancing.

citizen In ancient Rome, being a citizen gave a person a wide range of privileges, such as the right to vote or to stand for public office. Only free men could be Roman citizens.

Colosseum The name since medieval times of a vast amphitheater in Rome, completed in 81CE. The Romans knew it as the Flavian Amphitheatre.

dysentery An infection of the intestines that causes severe diarrhea.

fenugreek A white-flowered plant of the pea family with seeds that are used today for flavoring (and by the Romans as a medicine).

forceps A pair of pincers or tweezers used in surgery.

Forum The main public square in Rome, used at various times in the city's history for triumphal processions, elections, public speeches, criminal trials, gladiatorial matches, and as a marketplace. All Roman cities had a forum at their center.

hearth A fireplace.

hypogeum An underground chamber.

Judea The region that is modern-day Israel.

latrine A communal toilet.

lyre A stringed instrument like a small U-shaped harp.

monarchy A form of government with a king or queen at the head.

pumice stone A very light volcanic stone, full of tiny holes. It is formed when frothy lava rapidly becomes solid. It can be used as an abrasive to remove hard skin.

Renaissance The great revival of art and literature in the 14th–16th centuries, influenced by the rediscovery of ancient Greek and Roman works.

republic A form of government in which supreme power is held by the people and their elected representatives (senators in the case of ancient Rome).

Senate The main law-making assembly of ancient Rome.

senator A member of the Senate.

sewer An underground channel for carrying drainage water and waste matter.

vendor A street trader.

Vestal A priestess of the Roman goddess Vesta.

For More Information

WEBSITES

www.bbc.co.uk/schools/primaryhistory/romans/
This introduction to Ancient Rome has sections on the city of Rome, Roman Britain, the army, roads, leisure, family and children, technology, and religion.

www.brims.co.uk/romans/tutorial.html
This site provides articles on the Roman army, the invasion of Britain, Roman towns, homes, gods, buildings, food and farming, and clothes.

www.museumoflondon.org.uk/Resources/learning/digging/index.html
This site explores ancient Roman life through archaeological remains. It explores Roman people, town life, invasion and settlement, army, beliefs, crafts, roads, and trade.

www.pbs.org/empires/romans/empire/index.html
This site looks at the history of Rome, daily life, the structure of Roman society, the emperors, great Roman writers, Roman religion, and enemies and rebels of Rome.

http://www.roman-empire.net/children/index.html
This site offers sections on Roman history, buildings, great achievements, famous Romans and Roman gods, as well as an interesting section on the "evils of Rome," which looks at slavery, gladiatorial games, and cruel emperors.

BOOKS

Ancient Romans (Hail!) by Philip Steel (Wayland, 2013)

Ancient Rome (Fact Files) by Fiona MacDonald, Rupert Matthews and Philip Steele (Miles Kelly, 2012)

Ancient Rome (Visitor's Guides) by Lesley Sims (author) and Christyan Fox (illustrator) (Usborne, 2014)

Race Through Rome (History Quest) by Timothy Knapman (QED Publishing, 2013)

The Roman Colosseum (Spectacular Visual Guides) by Fiona MacDonald (author) and Mark Bergin (illustrator) (Book House, 2010)

Rome (Picturing the Past) by Richard Dargie (Franklin Watts, 2007)

Index